Texas State Capitol

Jane Moorman

There is a saying, "It was a Friday night and it seemed like a good idea at the time." That sums up the beginning of the State Capitols Project.

When I told my brother of my idea of photographing state capitols, he said, "You do know there are 50 states and two of them you can't drive to."

Each capitol has its own unique beauty that reflects the state's personality when it was built.

Jane Moorman, photographer

Six Flags Over Texas

Texas uniquely honors its history of being a territory that was ruled by six different countries—Spain, France, Mexico, the Republic of Texas, the Confederate States of America, and the United States.

When architect Elijah E. Myers of Detroit designed the state capitol, this part of Texas's history was honored in several places— above the north and south entrances and on the "Seals of the Nations" in the center of the rotunda floor.

The present building was constructed between 1882 and 1888, showcasing the capitol's Renaissance Revival style, which was inspired by the National Capitol in Washington, D.C.

The Texas government paid for the construction of the building with three million acres of public land in the Texas Panhandle, which later became known as the renowned XIT Ranch.

The original plans called for the capitol's exterior to be native limestone, but all of the limestone found near Austin contained discoloring iron particles. The contractor proposed using limestone from Indiana, but Governor John Ireland wished to use Texas stone, specifically red granite from Granite Mountain near Marble Falls.

After labor difficulties arose in 1886, stemming from the use of prison convict labor to quarry the granite, stone cutters from Scotland were brought in for the work.

Work began on the iron dome in mid-1887, and the Goddess of Liberty was hoisted to the top of it in February 1888. The building was dedicated in May 1888.

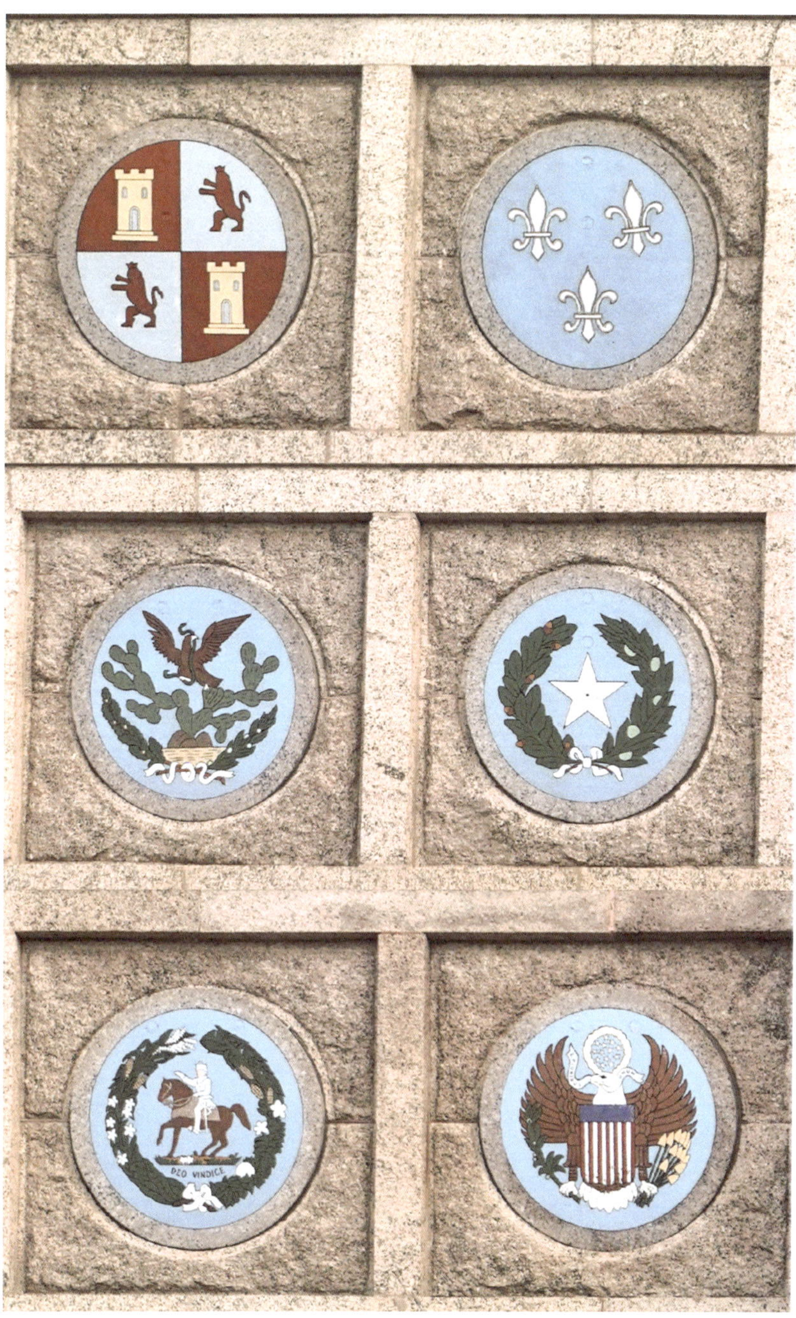

Sunset Red Texas Granite

Elijah E. Myers, architect of the Michigan and Colorado capitols, designed the Renaissance Revival style building. The structure was completed with the superb Sunset Red Texas Granite that makes the building so distinctive.

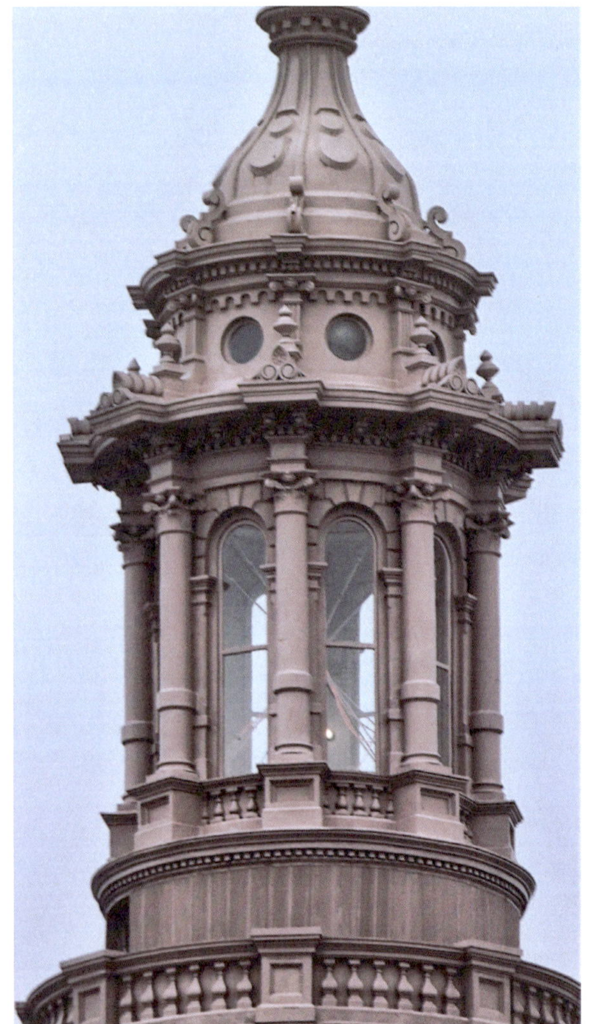

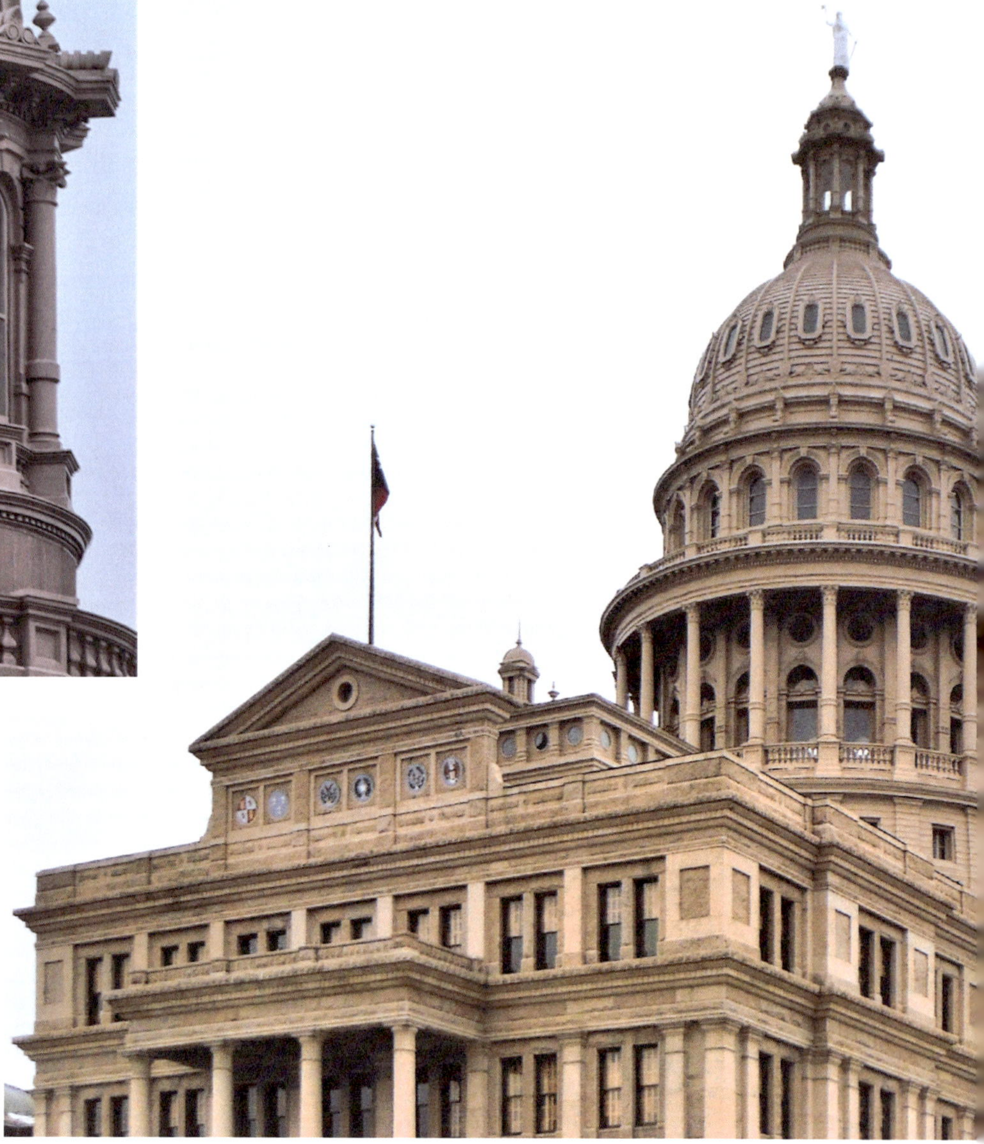

Approximately 188,000 cubic feet of granite, quarried 50 miles northwest of Austin near Marble Falls, was transported by a specially built railroad and teams of oxen.

The owner of Granite Mountain generously offered the building stone free of charge to the state.

Goddess of Liberty

In February 1888, the original 15-feet, 7.5-inches tall zinc Goddess of Liberty was placed atop the dome. The tip of the star reaches 302.64 feet above the ground.

It was replaced with an aluminum duplicate in 1984. The original Goddess of Liberty is a permanent exhibit at the Bullock Texas State History Museum.

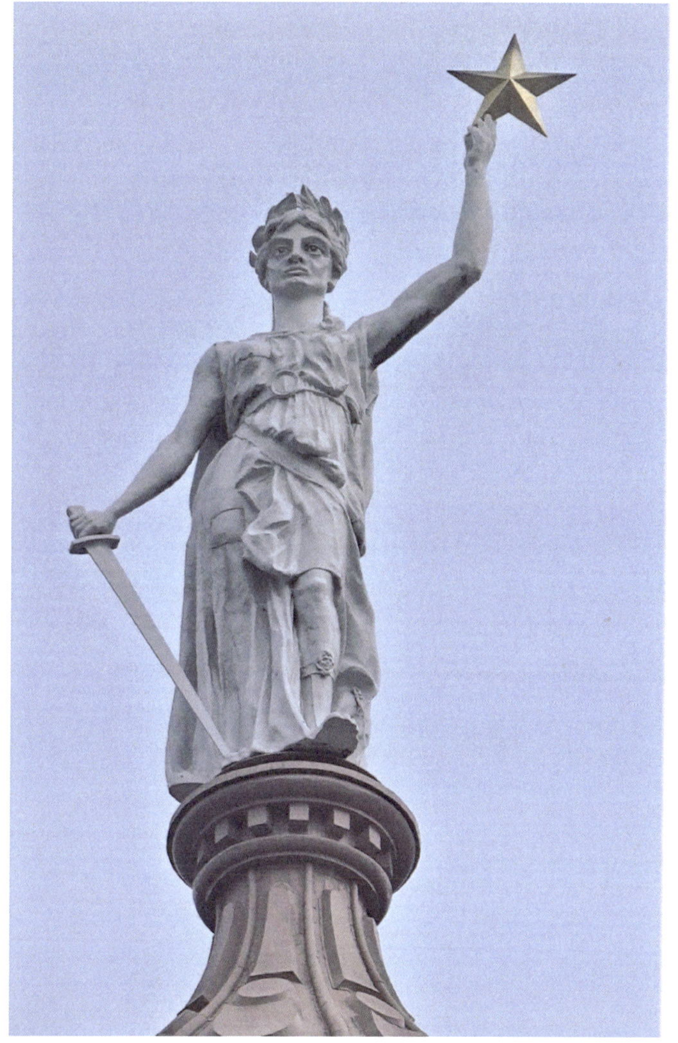

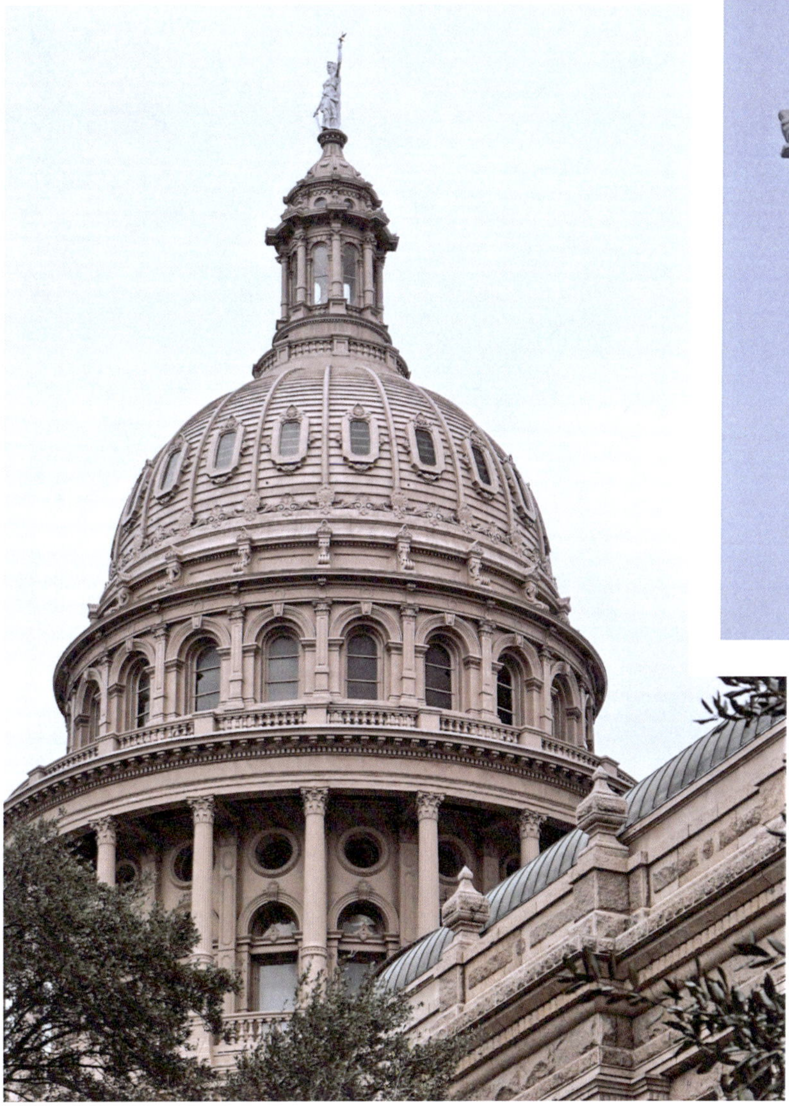

Likely inspired by the Statue of Freedom on top of the U.S. Capitol and the Statue of Liberty being built in New York City harbor at the time, architect Elijah Myers designed the Goddess of Liberty. The star symbolizes the pride and go-it-alone spirit of the independent republic that is still part of the Texas way of life.

Rotunda Dome

The rotunda measures 266 feet from the terrazzo star on the floor to the bronze star in the inner dome crown.

A huge sheet metal star, measuring 8 feet from point to point, has letters between each point that spell "Texas."

The four upper floors of the Capitol overlook the rotunda, where portraits of the four presidents of the Republic of Texas and past governors of the State of Texas are displayed along the walls of each floor.

The rotunda's shape creates a "whispering gallery," a phenomenon in which faint sounds echoing across the dome may be heard on the opposite side.

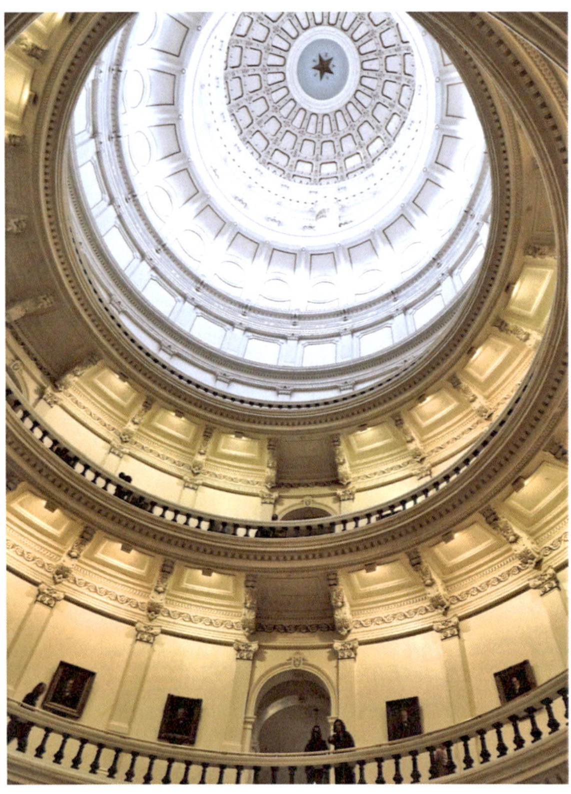

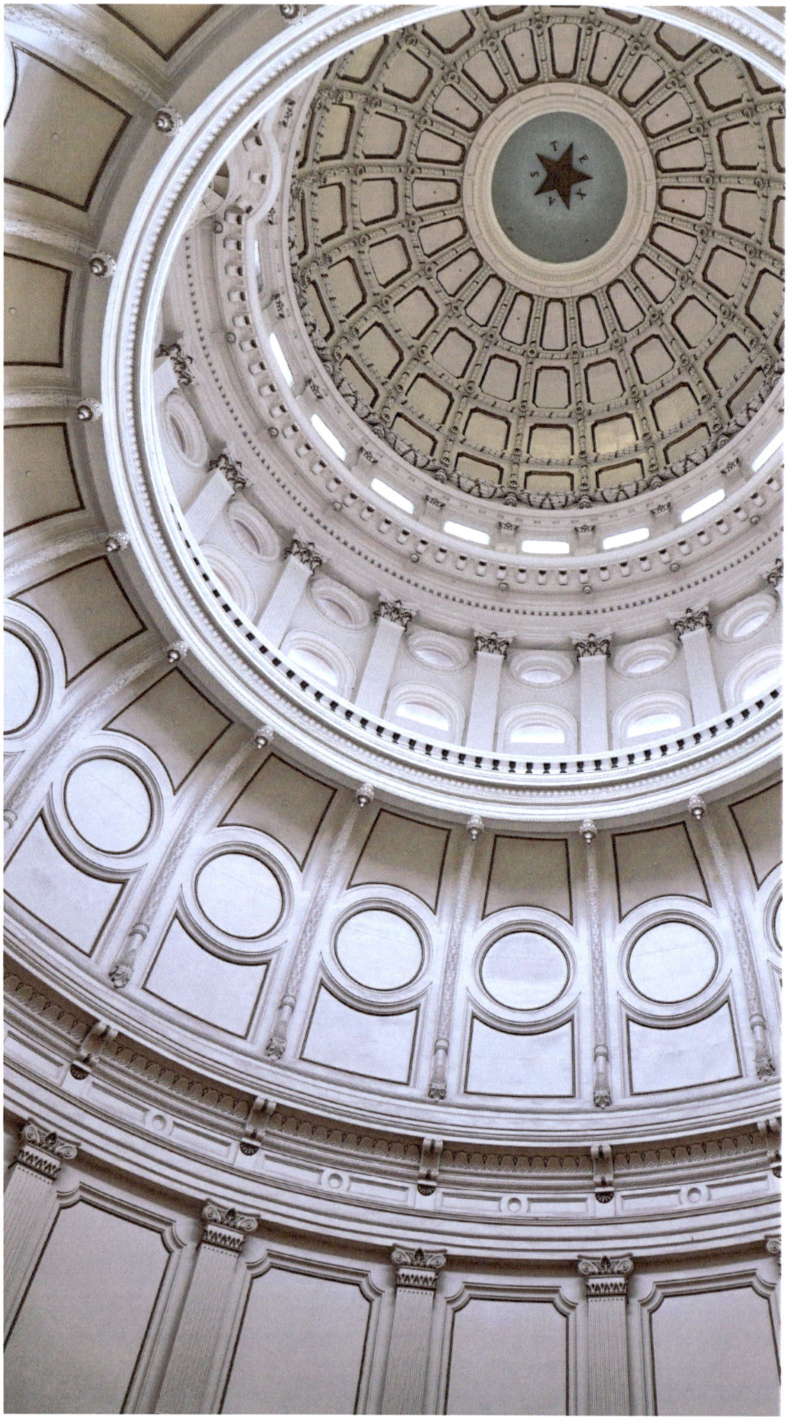

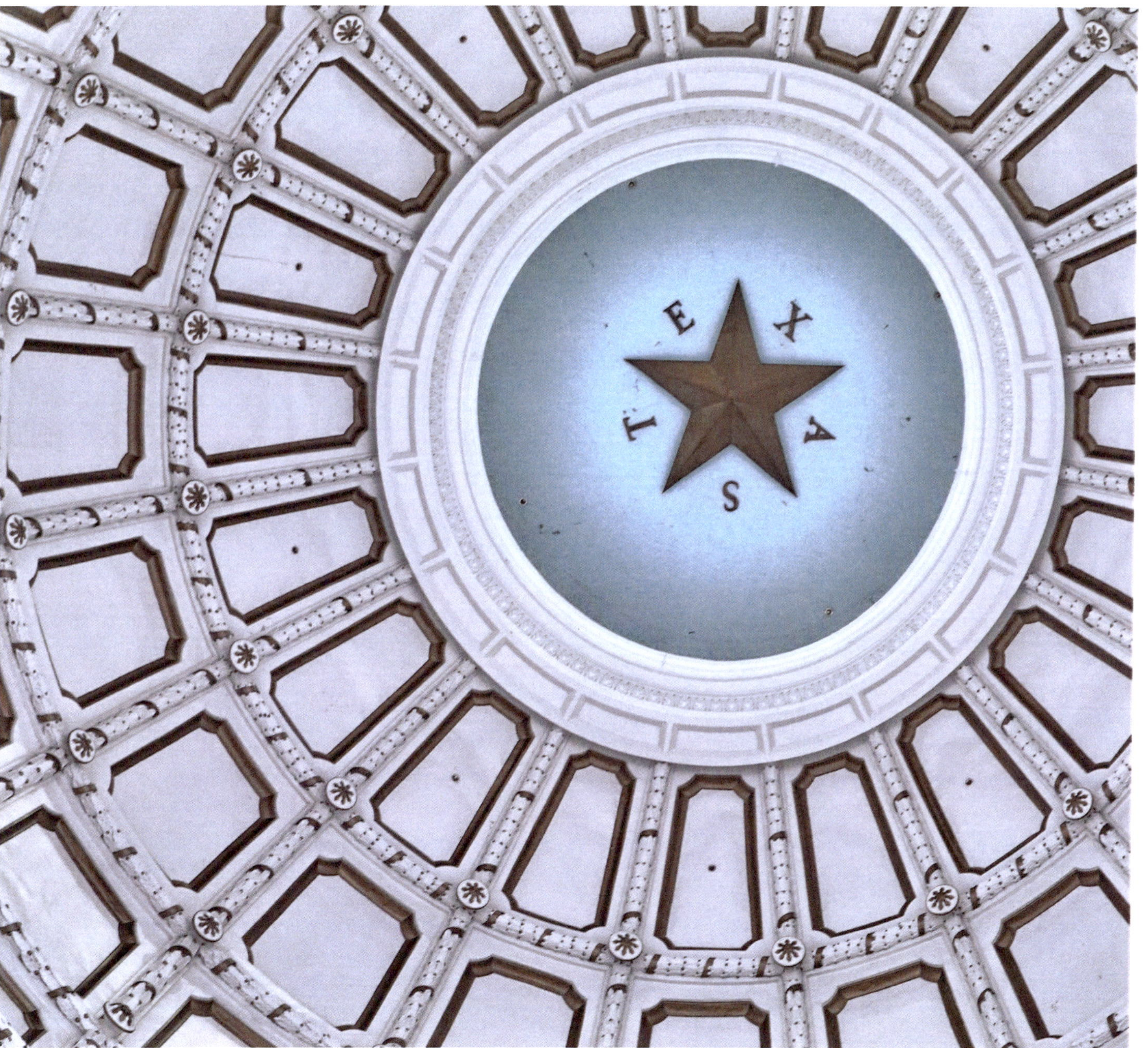

TEXAS

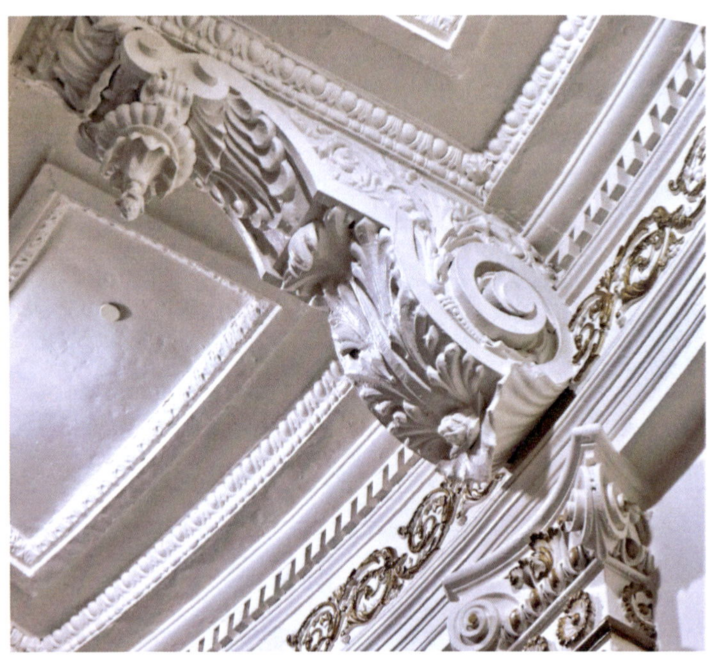
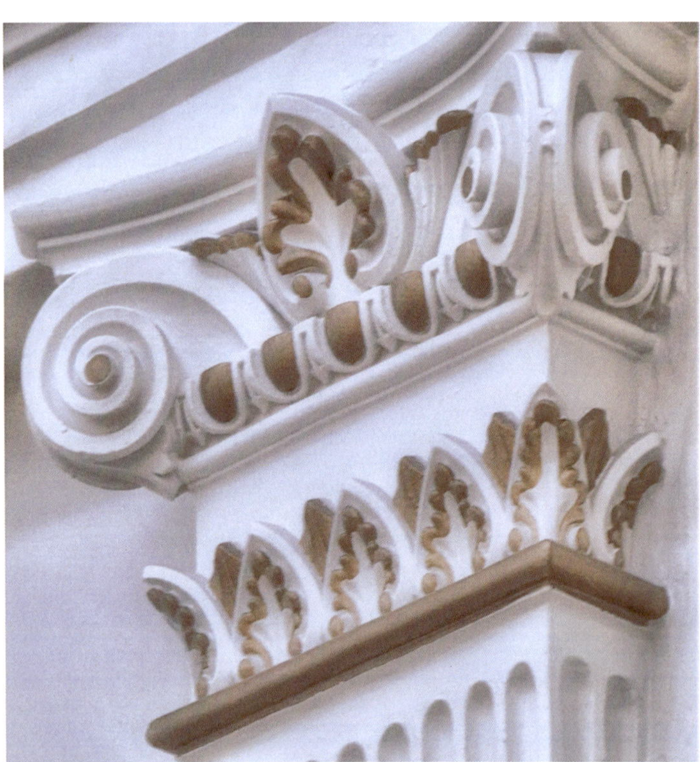

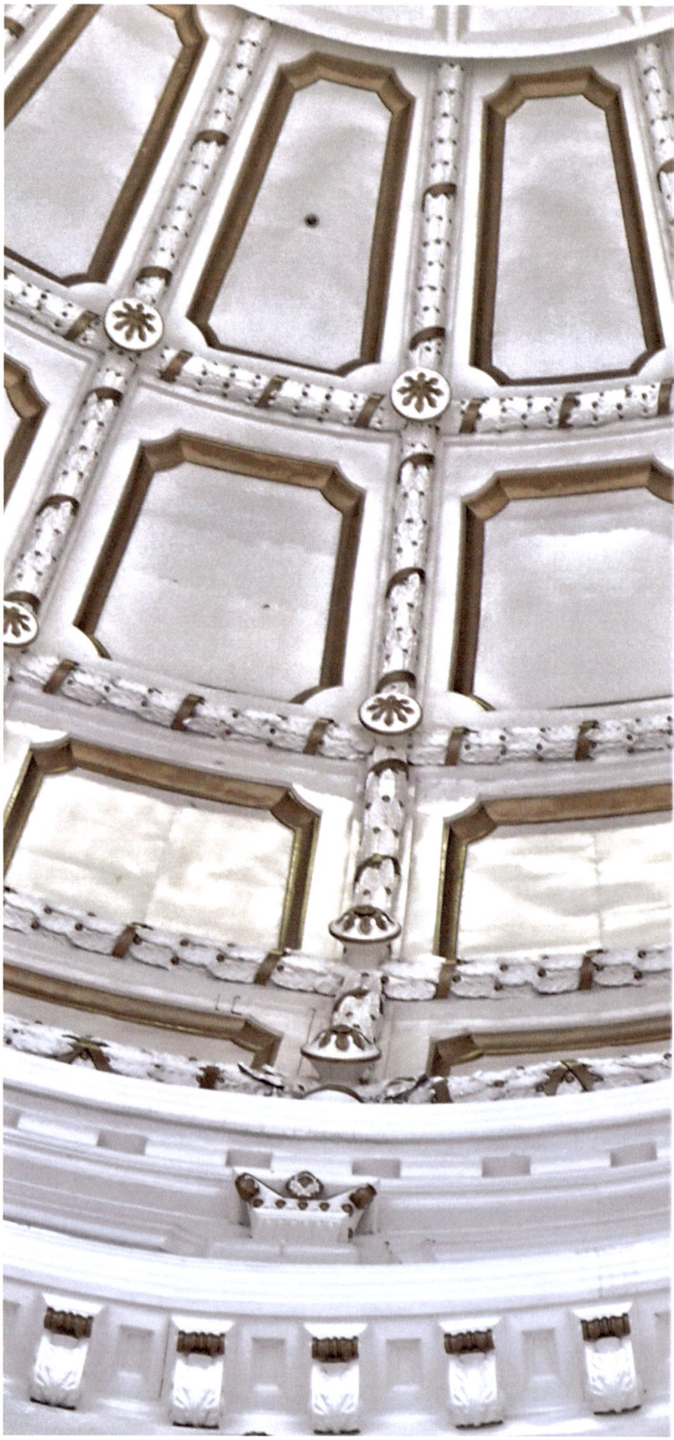

Rotunda Floor

A colorful terrazzo stonework design of the "Seals of the Nations" is in the center of the rotunda floor. The Seal of the Republic of Texas, with its iconic Lone Star, serves as the focal point of the giant pattern. Encircling the core and between the points of a larger star are the coats of arms from the five other nations of which Texas has been a part in history.

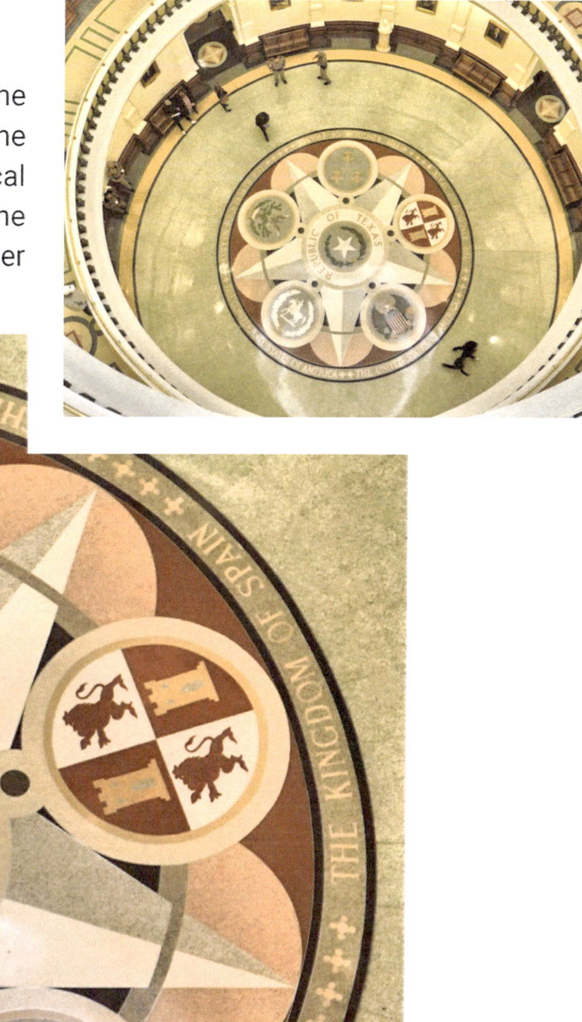

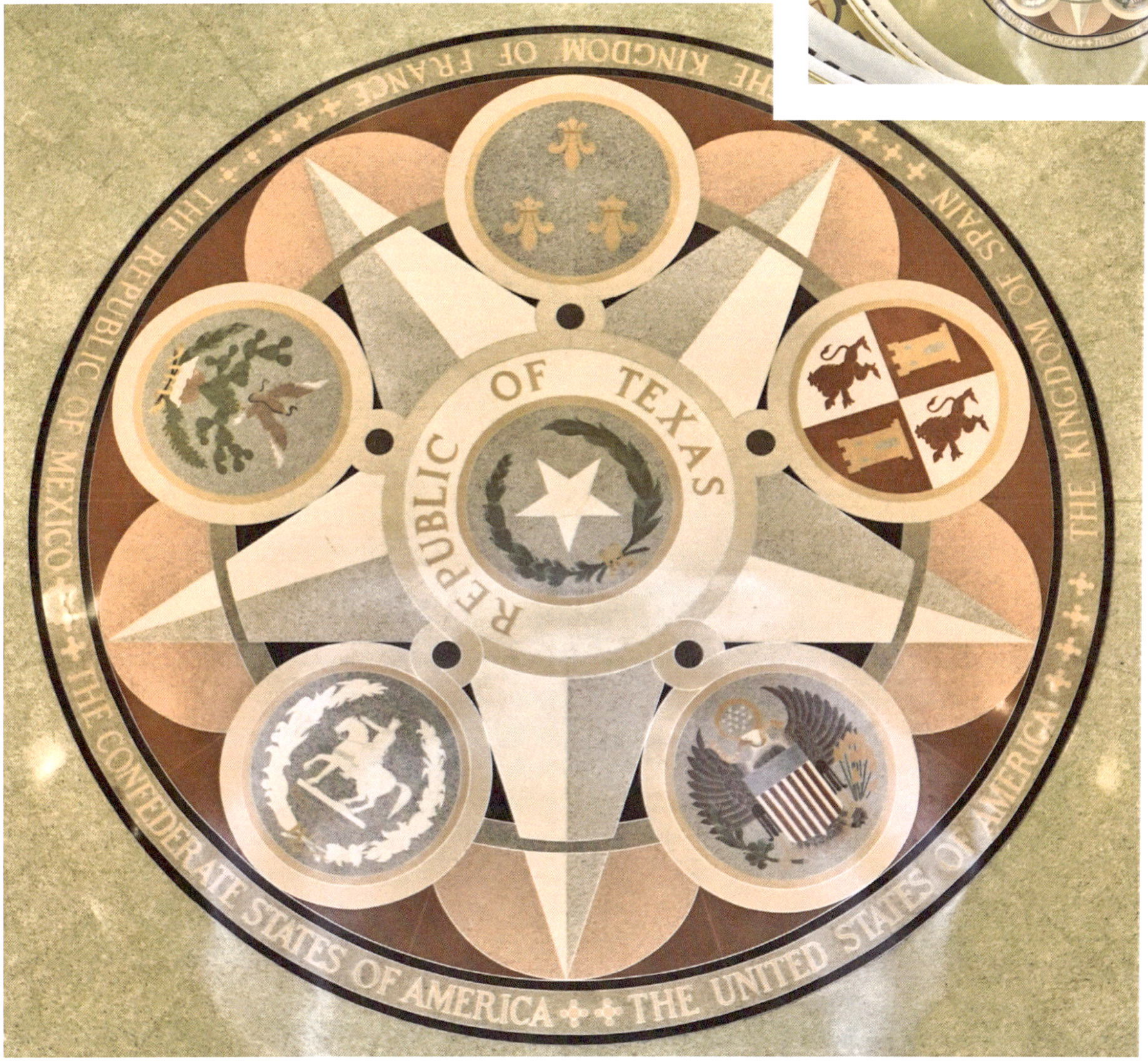

Grand Stairway

Ornately painted cast-iron staircases from Belgium flank the rotunda connecting the first and second floors.

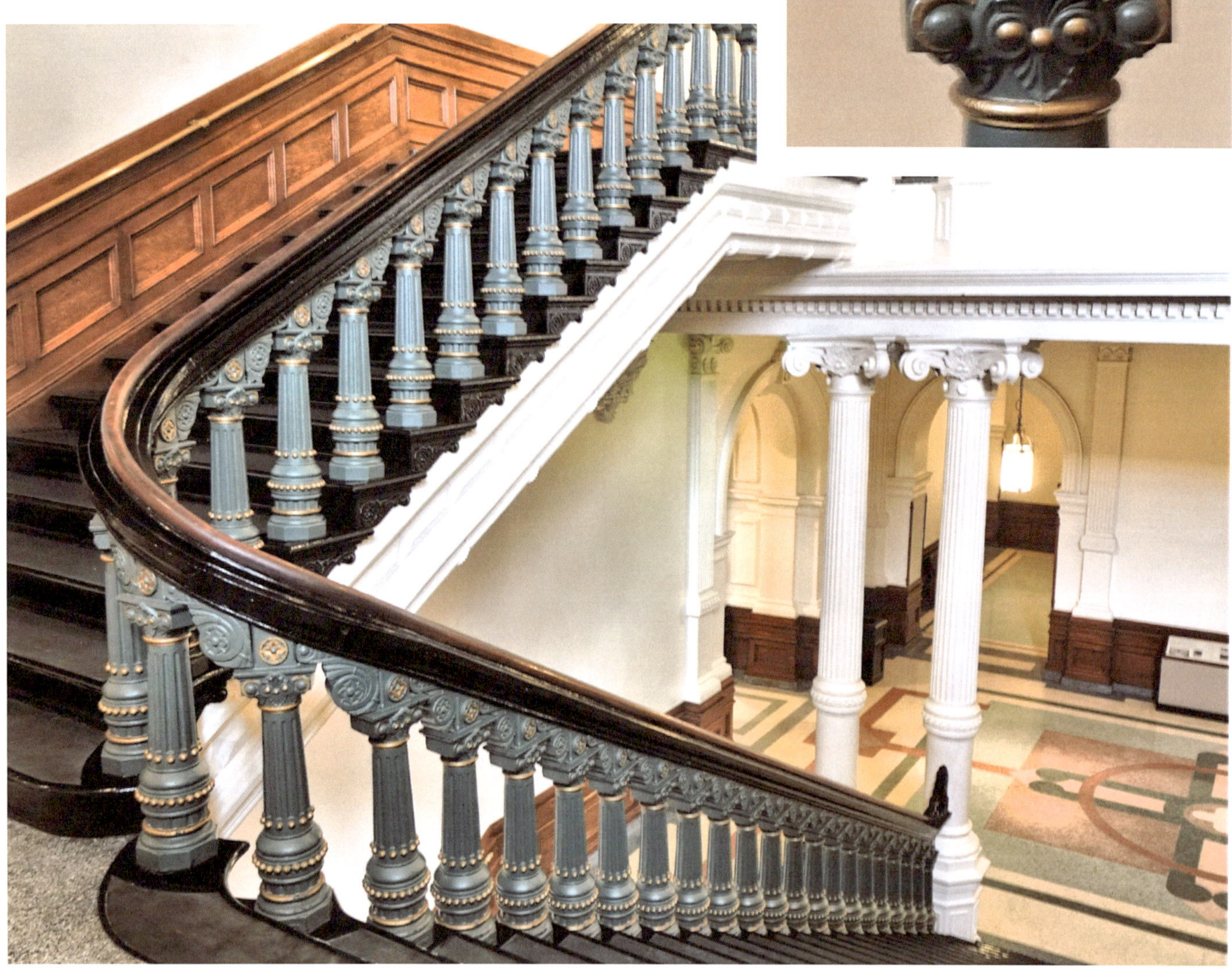

House of Representatives Chamber

The House Chamber, like the Senate, is one of the few rooms still used for its original purpose. Behind the rostrum used by the Speaker of the House hangs the original San Jacinto battle flag, which was carried by Texas at the decisive battle of the Texas Revolution. When the legislature is not in session, a reproduction flag hangs in its place so the original can be kept in darkness behind the drapery.

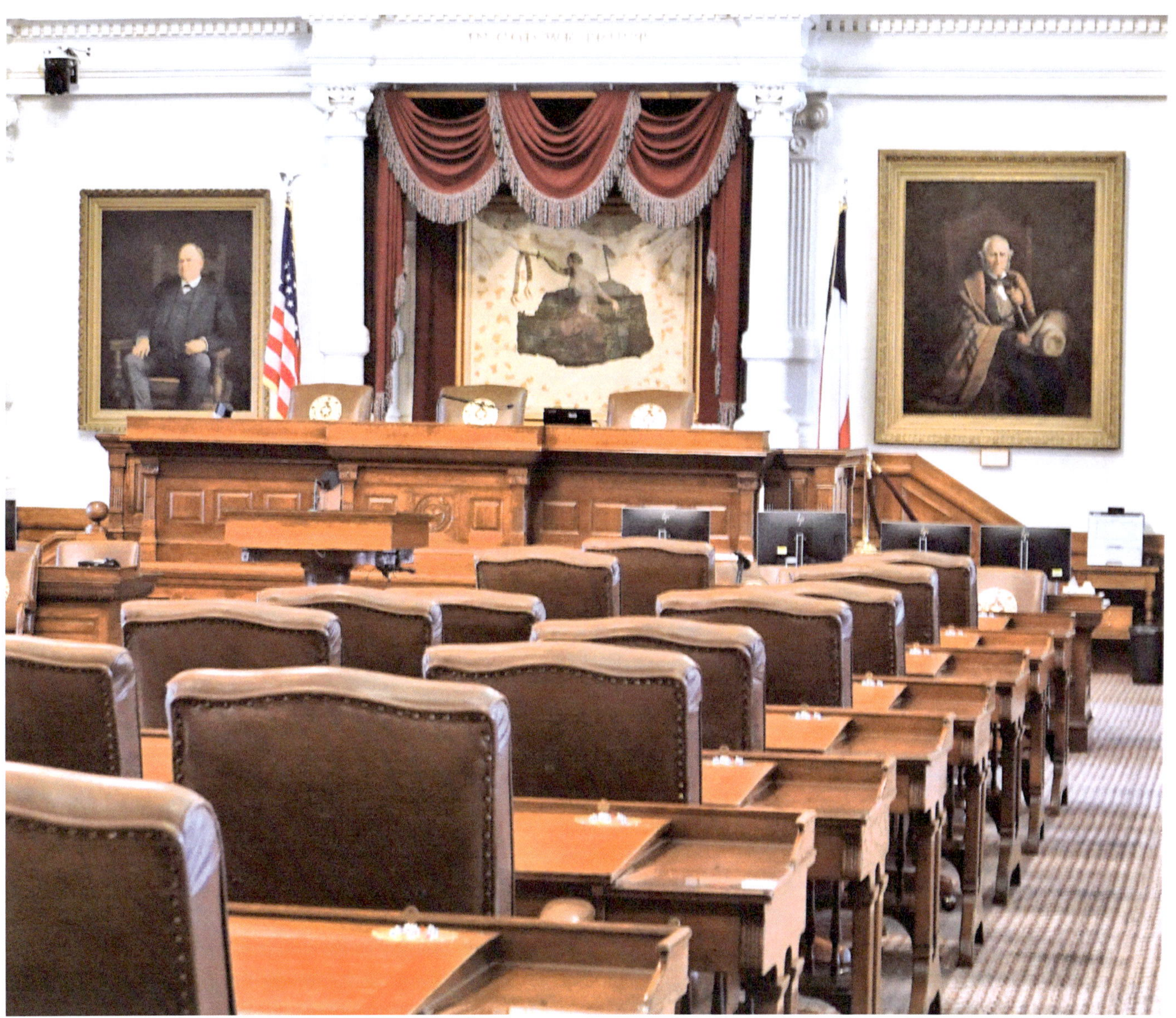

Henry Arthur McArdle Paintings in Senate Chamber

Henry Arthur McArdle conducted comprehensive research on the two key battles of the Texas Revolution to create the eight-feet by thirteen-feet paintings. However, the works of art do not depict absolute historical facts.

Dawn at the Alamo, painted in 1905, shows celebrated Alamo defenders, including David Crocket swinging "Old Besty" in the lower right corner, the ailing James Bowie using his trademark knife in the lower left corner and Commander William B. Travis being stabbed in the back in the upper right corner.

Battle of San Jacinto, painted in 1895, shows the final battle of the revolution, where 900 Texas soldiers defeated a much larger Mexican force.

McArdle painted many of the faces from photographs or from his memory.

He designed the painting with the viewer in mind, allowing them to grasp the magnitude of the battle at a glance while also appreciating the details.

Dawn at the Alamo

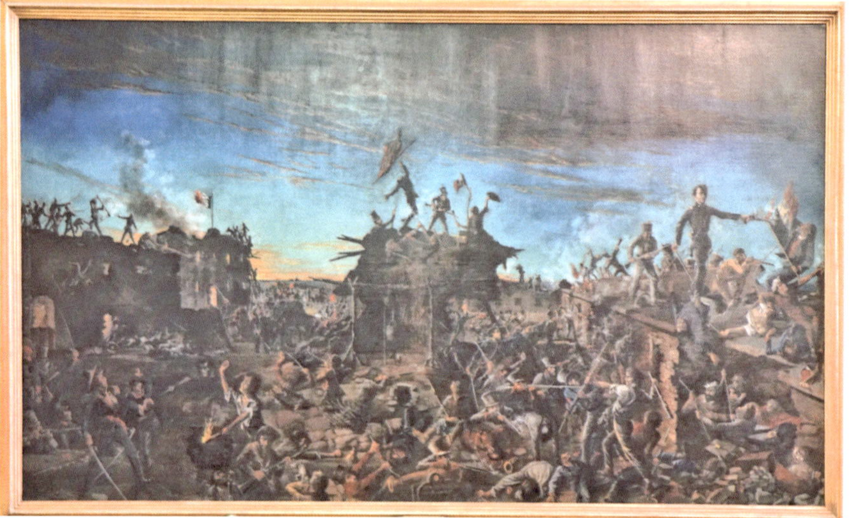

Battle of San Jacinto

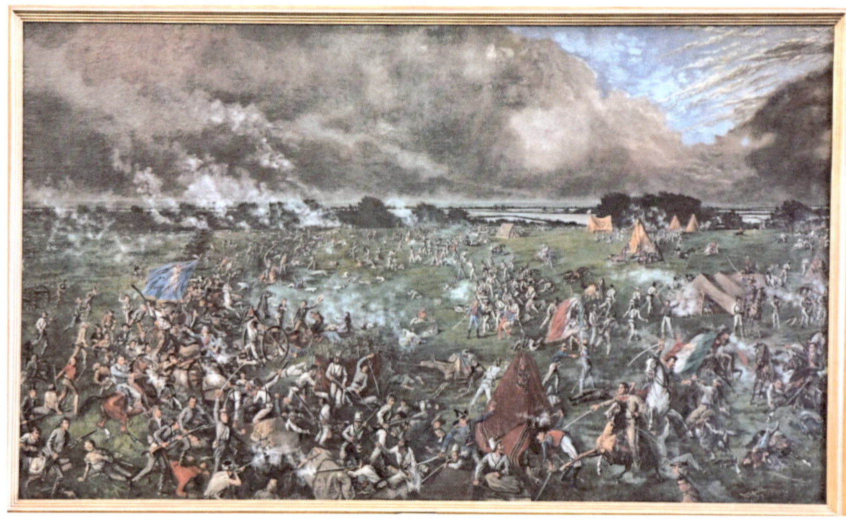

Senate Chamber

The Senate Chamber includes an impressive collection of historical Texas paintings, fifteen of which hung in the room before 1915. A portrait by an unknown artist of Stephen F. Austin, who was known as the "Father of Anglo Texas," behind the Lieutenant Governor's desk dates from c. 1836, making it one of the oldest pieces in the capitol.

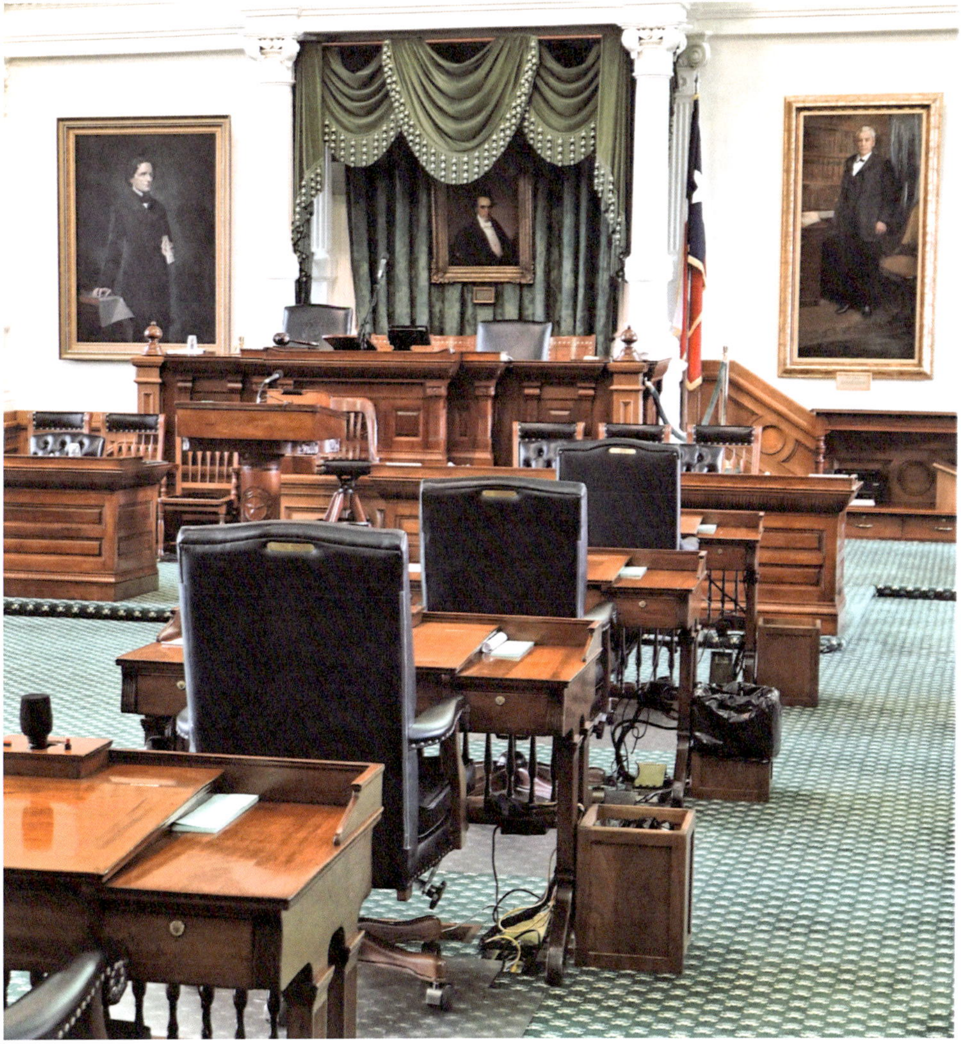

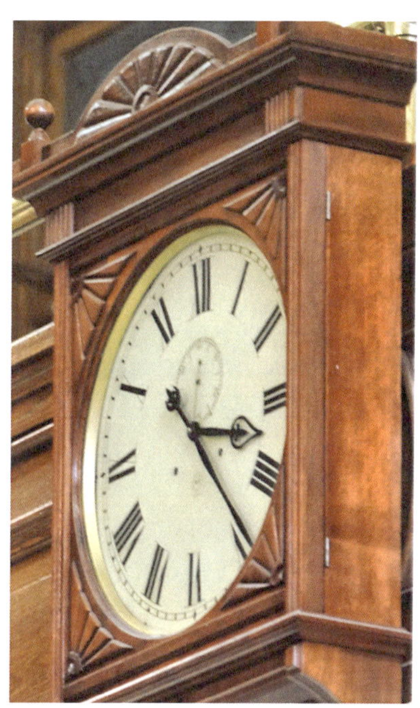

Chamber Chandeliers

Two beautiful central brass chandeliers dating from around 1890 provide light in the Senate.

Each chandelier features the Lone Star with the letters T. E. X. A. S; the lights of one chandelier spell out the word.

The ceiling glass panels have an etched Lone Star motif.

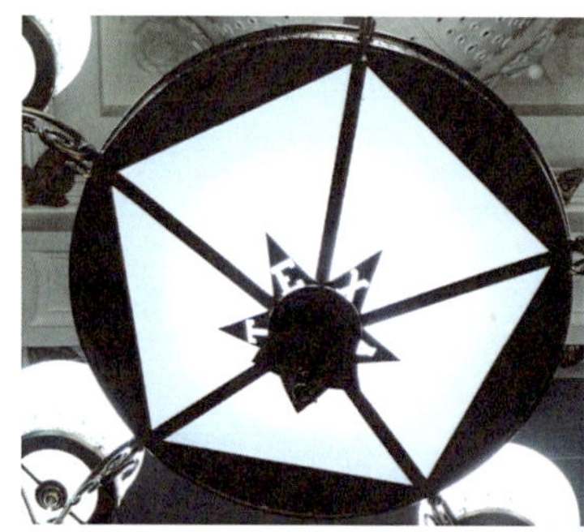

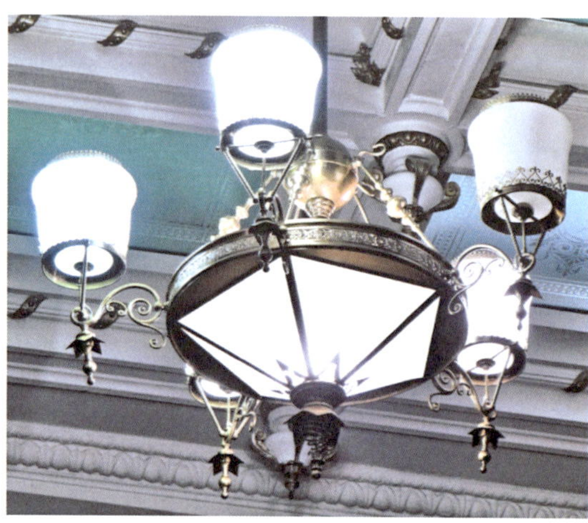

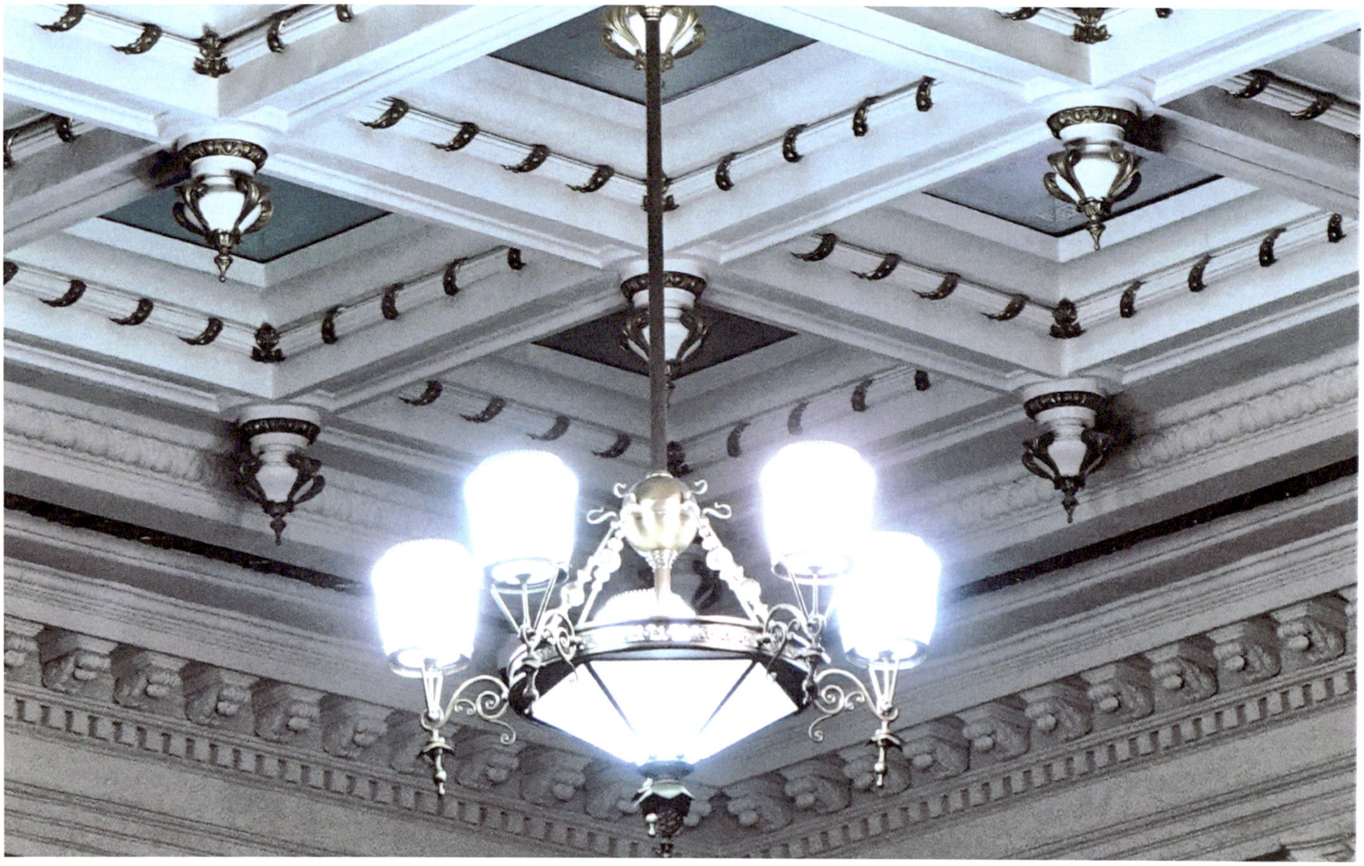

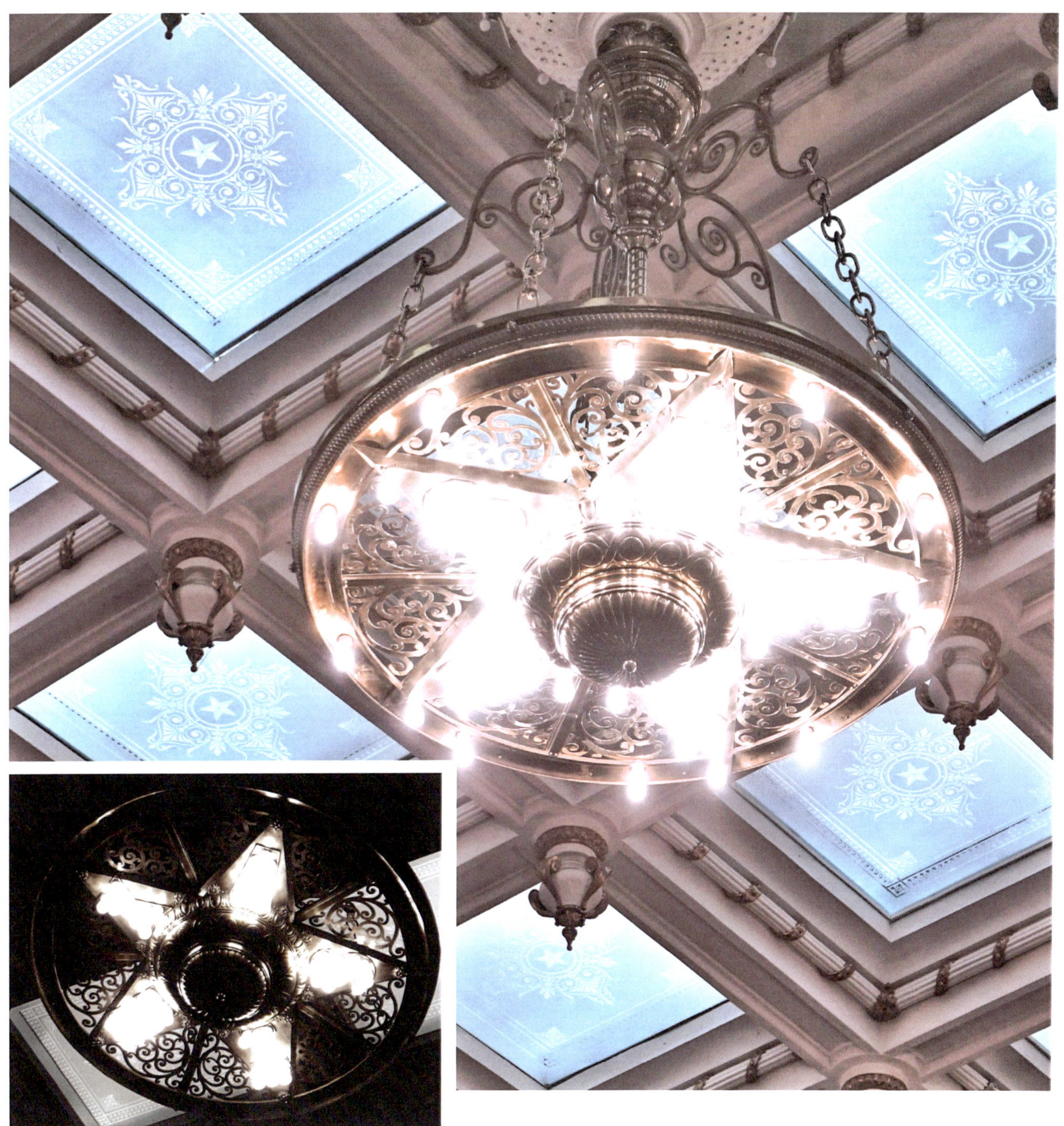

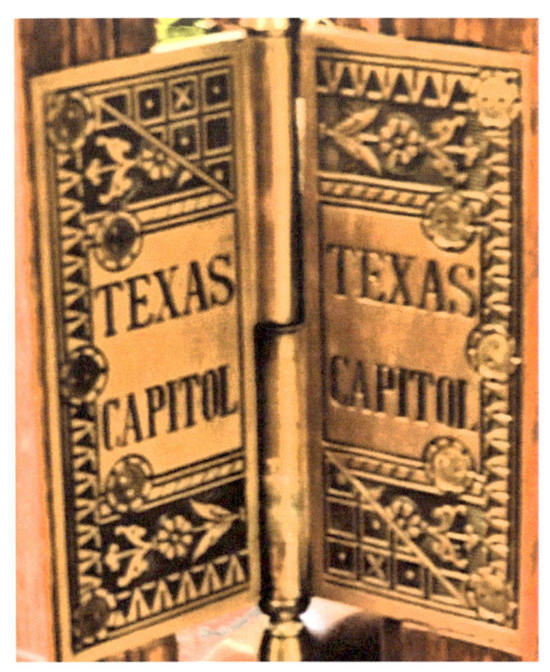

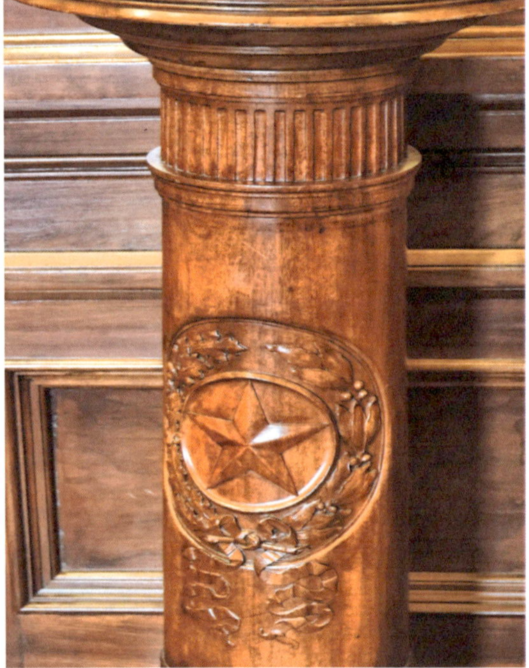

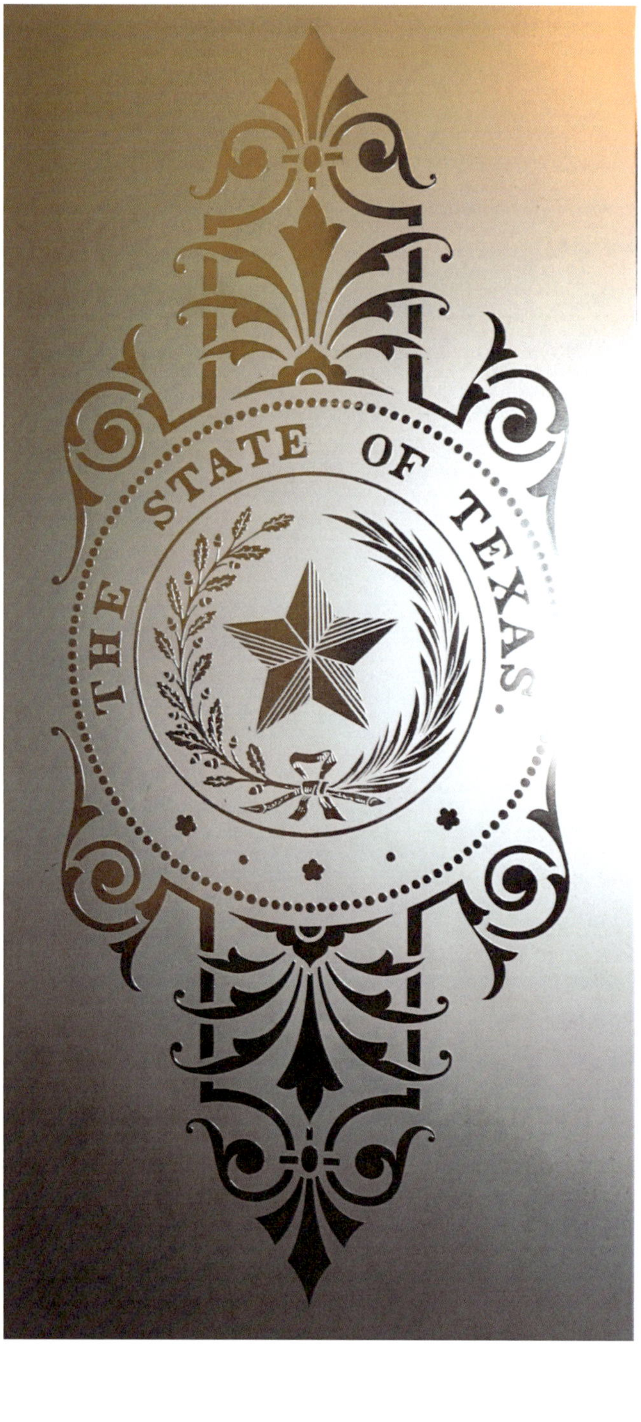

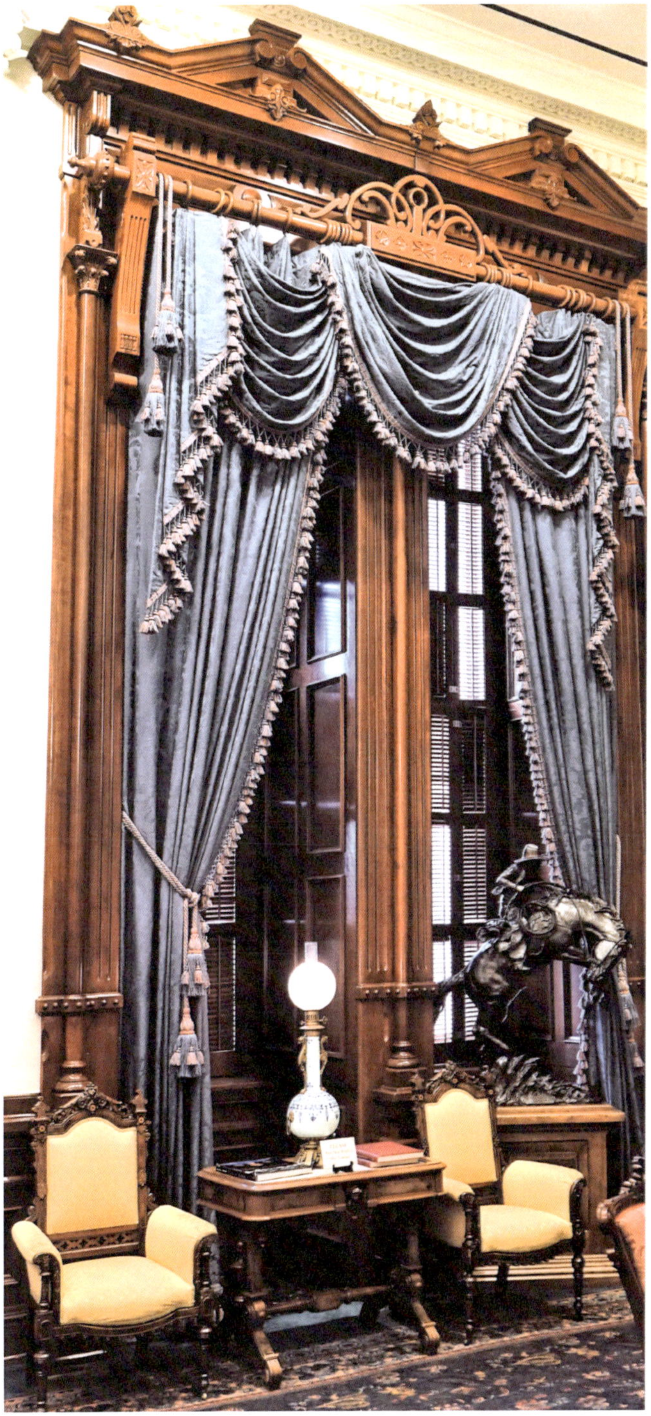

Governor's Reception

The Texas Governor uses the Reception Room on the second floor for ceremonial occasions and to greet distinguished guests. The room is furnished with handsome, late-19-century Victorian antiques, a few of which are original to the room, including the two plant stands and the brass chandelier.

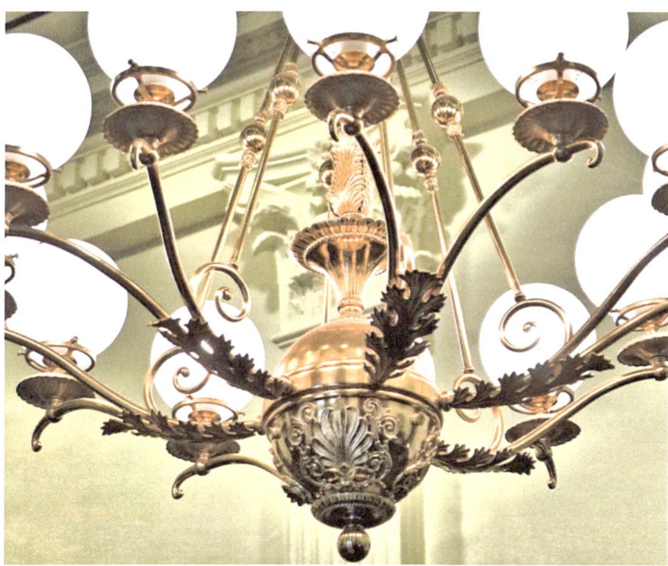

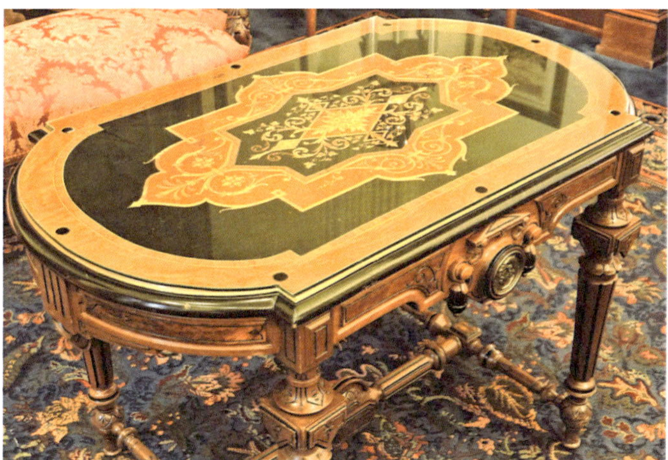

Terrazzo Floors

Terrazzo floors featuring geometric-patterned uses tile, glass tile, marble, wood, and concrete were originally laid on the first floor and rotunda in 1936; terrazzo on the upper floors were laid circa 1950s.

All terrazzo colors were created using Texas rock aggregate except for a small amount of white marble from Georgia.

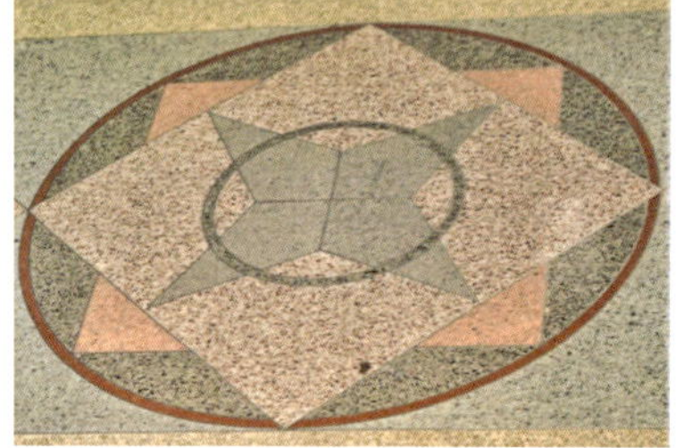

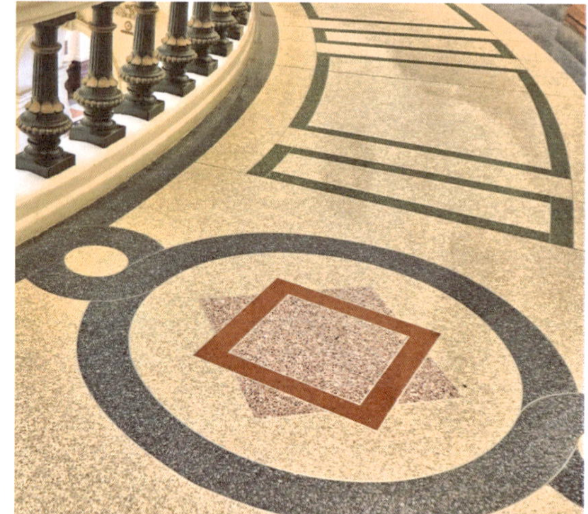

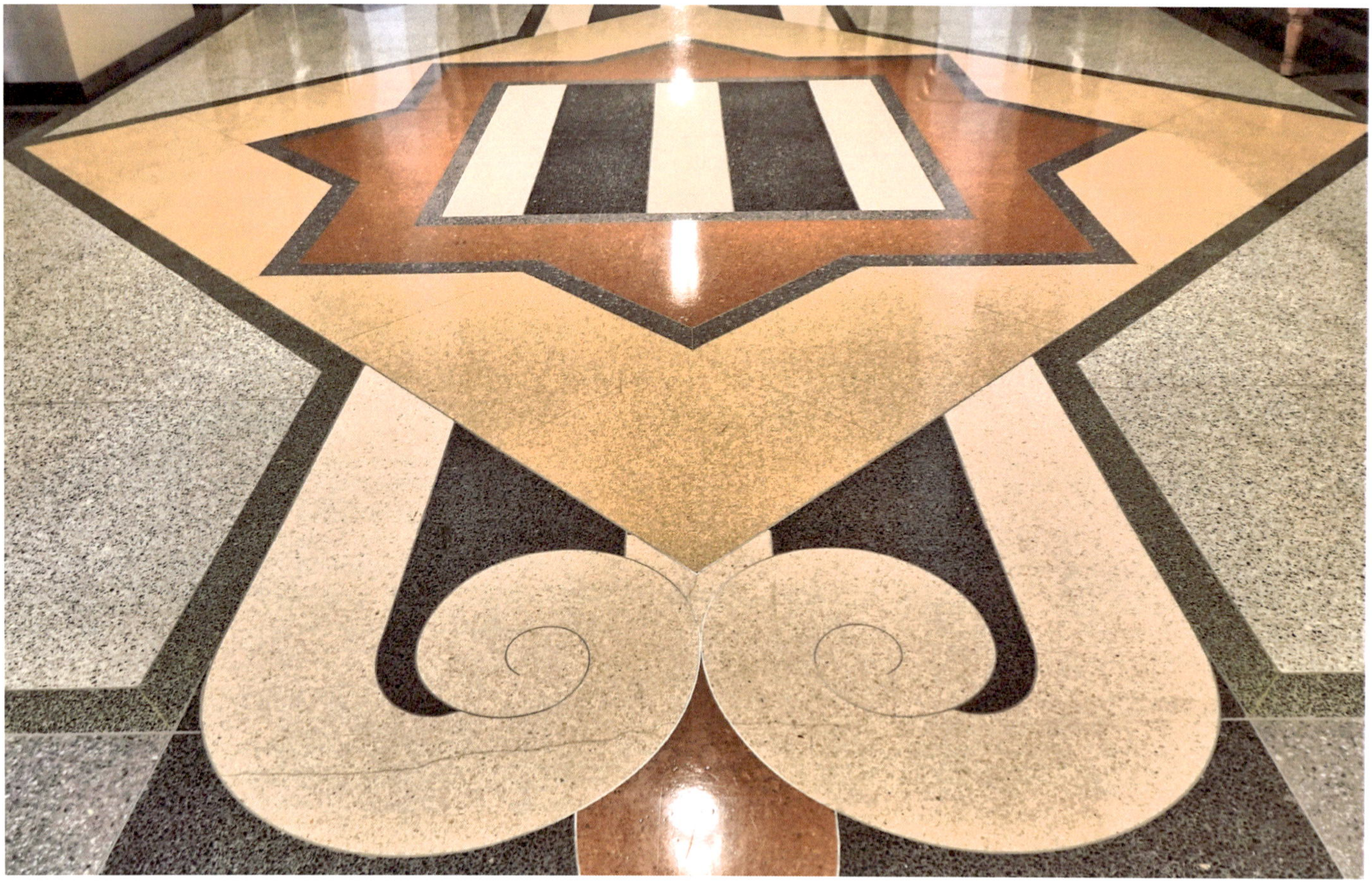

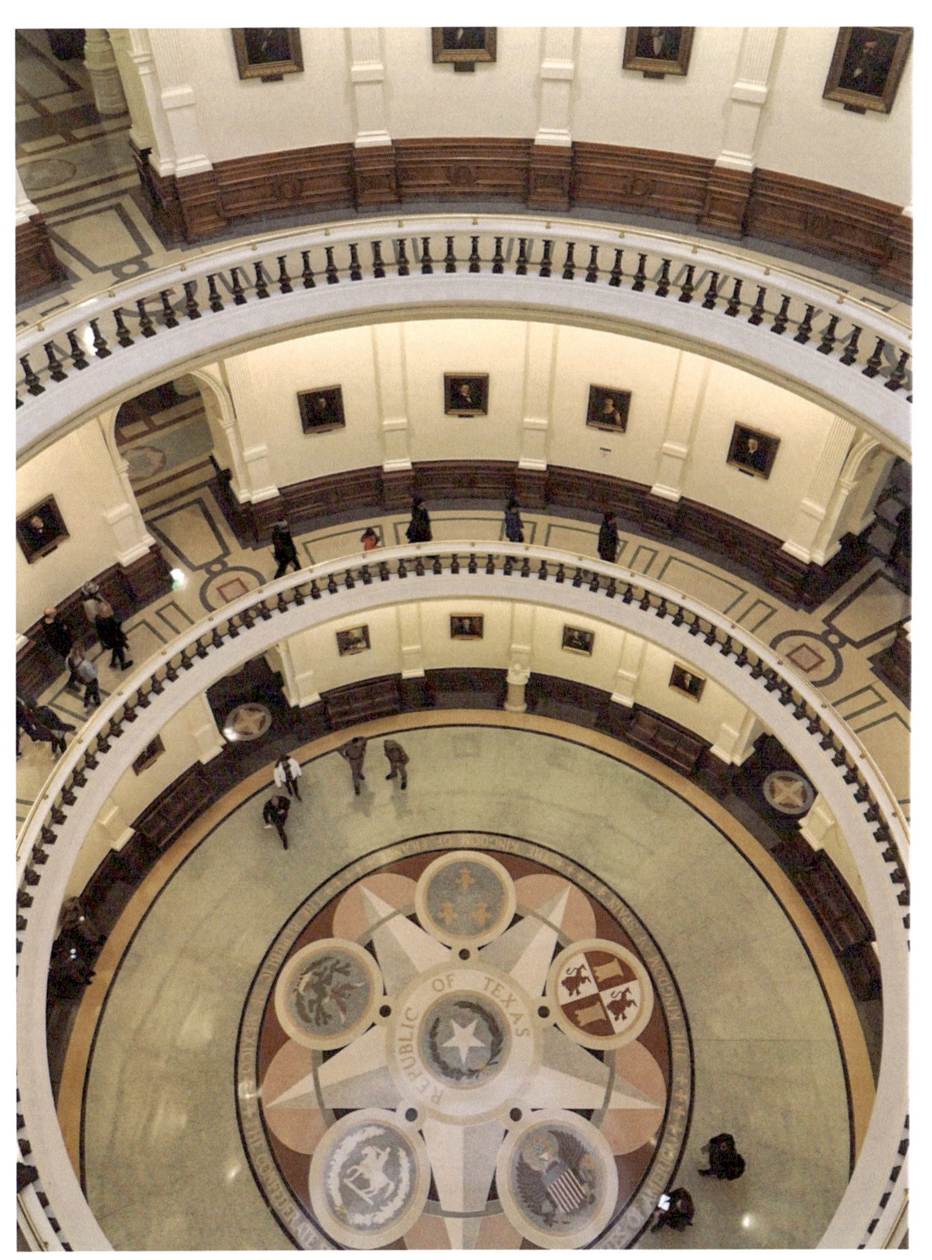

Governor Portraits

Portraits of the state's governors are displayed on the walls of the three floors of the rotunda. The most recent governors are on the first floor.

After a new governor is elected, staff members move the portraits one position to the right.

Brass Doorknobs, Plates

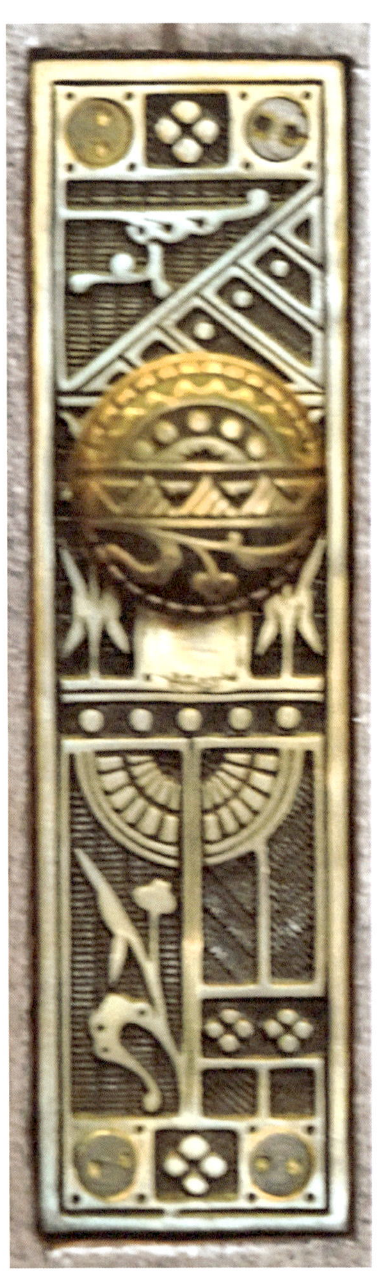 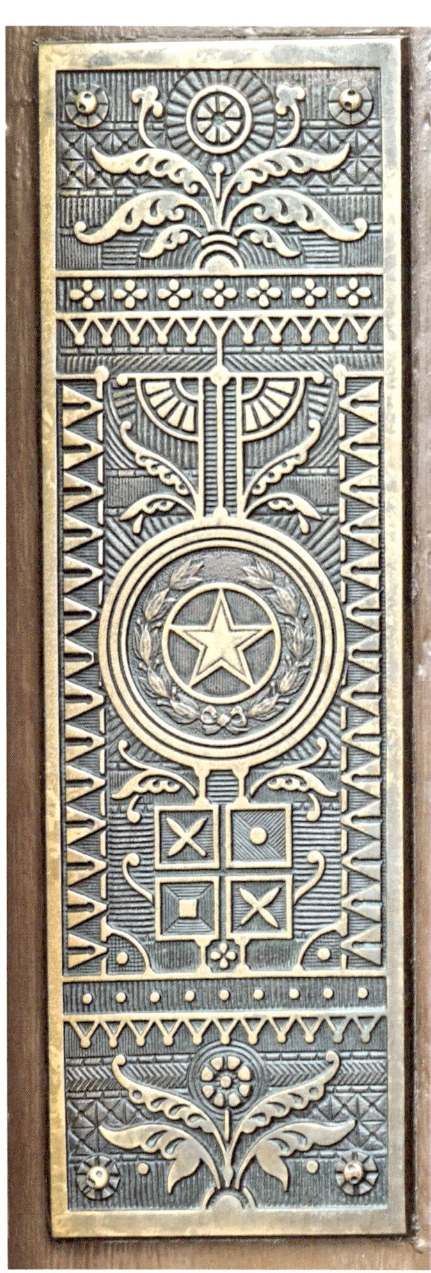 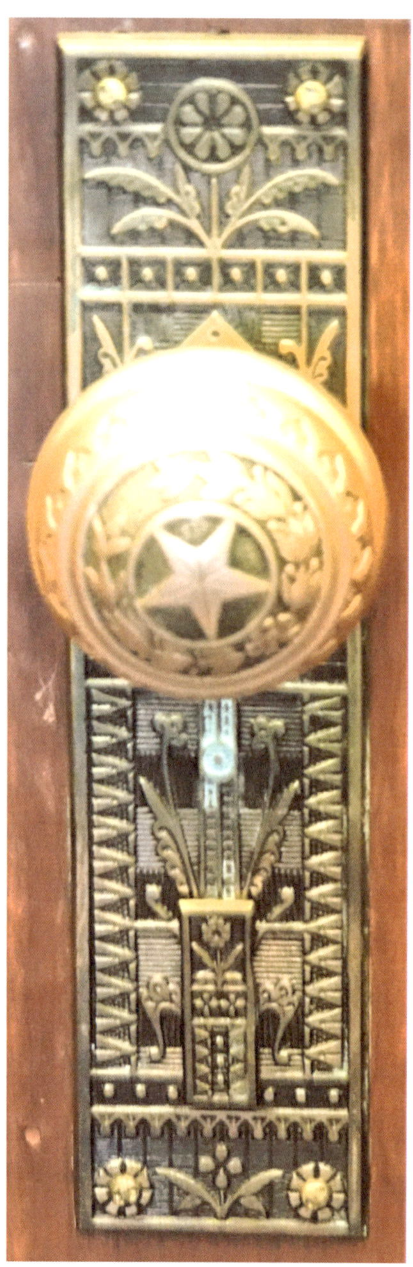

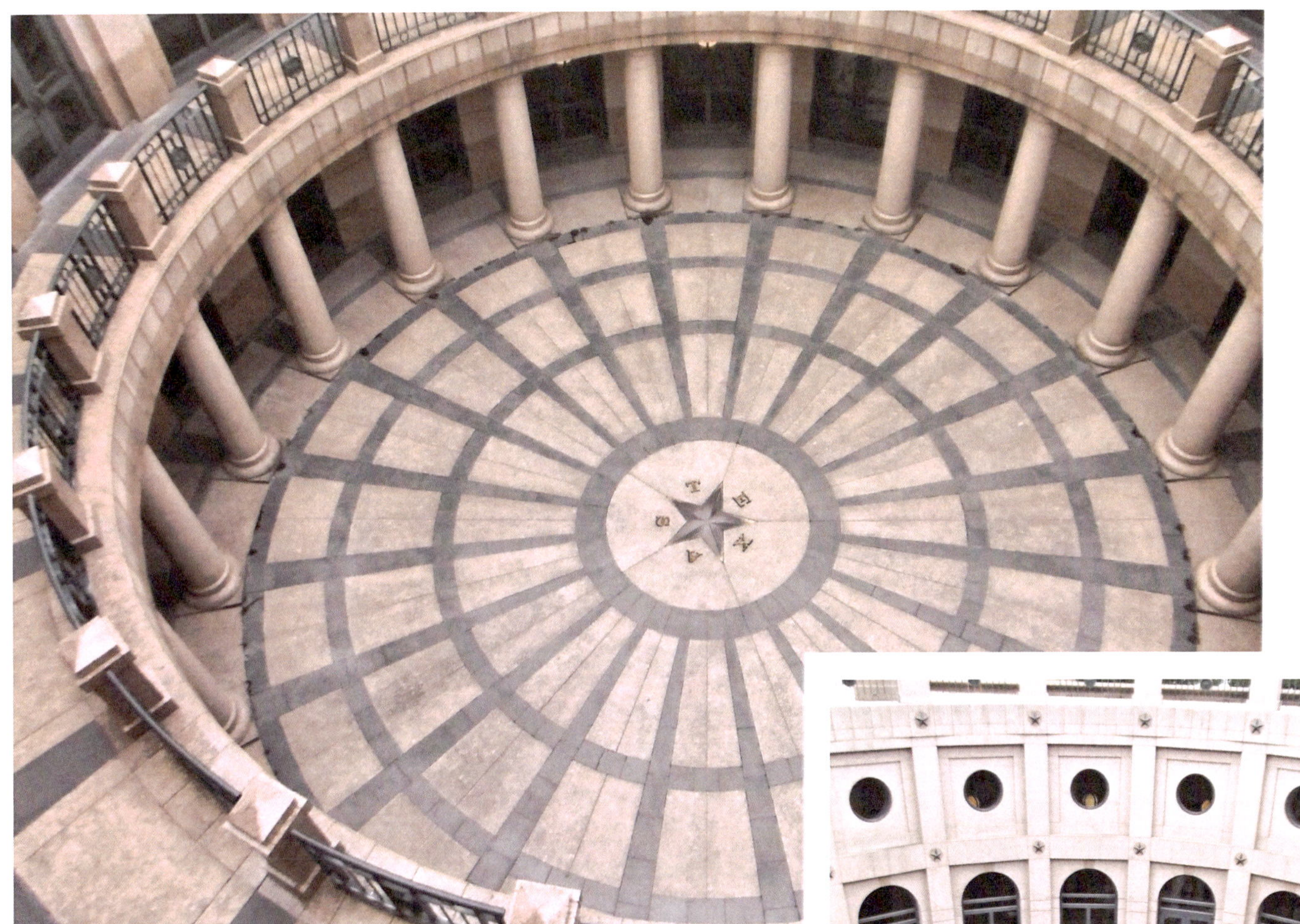

Building Extension Courtyard

As a part of the 1995 capitol renovations, a four-story underground Capitol Extension was built. This 650,000-square-foot extension is connected to the Capitol and five adjacent buildings by pedestrian tunnels.

The design of the two-story, open-air rotunda in the extension complements the Capitol rotunda. The bronze star on the floor reflects the style of the star in the ceiling of the Capitol dome. Both stars have letters between the points spelling out "Texas."

Texas State Seal: Uniquely Two Sided

The Seal of the State of Texas was adopted through the 1845 Texas Constitution and was based on the seal of the Republic of Texas, which dates from January 25, 1839.

The official artwork, created by Juan Vega of Round Rock, Texas, was adopted in 1992. It has specified working on both the obverse and reverse sides.

The seal has a five-point star encircled by olive and live oak branches and the words "The State of Texas."

On the reverse side, which was adopted in 1961, the seal has a more detailed design. Within a shield are three drawings reflecting the state's history. The upper half is the Alamo; the bottom left is a cannon of the Battle of Gonzales; and the bottom right is Vince's Bridge.

The shield is circled by live oak and olive branches and the unfurled flags of the Kingdom of France, the Kingdom of Spain, The United Mexican States, the Republic of Texas, the Confederate States of America and the United States of America.

Above the shield is emblazoned the motto, "Remember the Alamo," and beneath the shield are the words, "Texas One and Indivisible." Over the entire shield, centered between the flags, is a white five-pointed star.

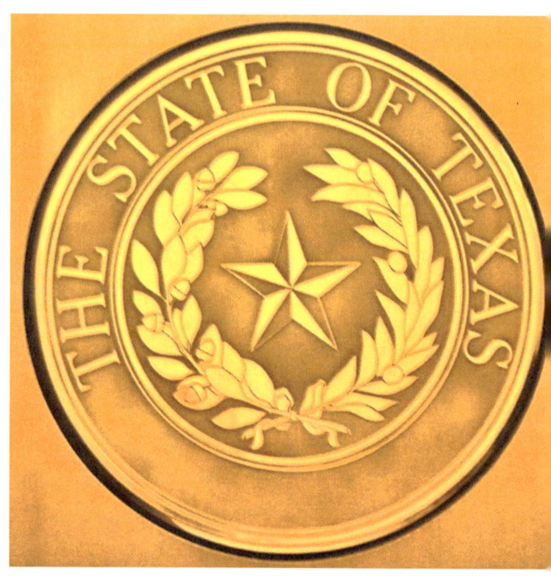

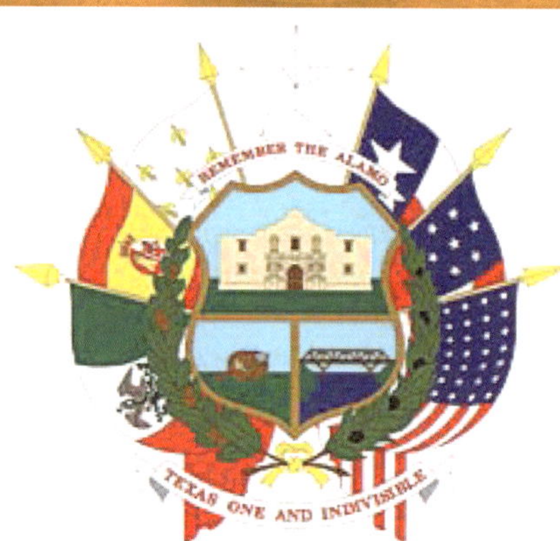

About the Photographer

Jane Moorman describes herself as an adventurer who loves to drive the backroads to see what there is to see.

During her 30-year journalism career, Jane honed her photographic skills as a photojournalist, including covering high school sporting events.

A friend once said, "I wish I could see the world as Jane sees it. Finding the beauty in things that most of us don't take time to see."

Upon retiring in 2021, Jane decided there was a lot of her native country she had not visited, including each state's capitol, so she began her journey of exploring the USA.

She currently lives in Albuquerque, New Mexico, but says her real home is on the road.